TAURUS HOROSCOPE & ASTROLOGY 2025

Mystic Cat

Suite 41906, 3/2237 Gold Coast HWY

Mermaid Beach, Queensland, 4218

Australia

islandauthor@hotmail.com

Copyright © 2023 by Mystic Cat

Time set to Coordinated Universal Time Zone (UT±0)

All rights reserved. This book or any portion thereof may not be reproduced or used in any manner without the publisher's express written permission except for the use of brief quotations in a book review.

The information accessible from this book is for informational purposes only. None of the data should be regarded as a promise of benefits. It should not be considered a statutory warranty or a guarantee of results achievable.

Images are used under license from Fotosearch & Dreamstime.

Contents

January	16
February	24
March	32
April	40
May	48
June	56
July	64
August	72
September	80
October	88
November	96
December	104

Hello there, Let me explain why my horoscope books may give different readings for each zodiac sign. The sky is always bustling with astrological activity, and I want to focus on what's most important for each star sign.

Every zodiac sign is unique, and the planets up above affect them differently. When I create horoscopes, I pay extra attention to the most critical astrological events for a specific sign. Some days, there might be lots of stuff happening in the stars, but one thing stands out as the essential factor for a particular zodiac sign.

I also consider which planet rules a sign and its associated element. This in-depth consideration helps me tailor my interpretations to match a sign's characteristics.

Ultimately, my goal is to provide you with unique advice and insights that match the cosmic influences for your sign. By focusing on what makes each sign special, I hope to help you understand yourself better and navigate the energies around you. Embracing your sign's strengths and challenges is the key to making my horoscopes feel uniquely aligned for you.

Cosmic Blessings,

Sia Sands

TAURUS 2025
HOROSCOPE & ASTROLOGY

Four Weeks Per Month

Week 1 – Days 1 - 7

Week 2 – Days 8 - 14

Week 3 – Days 15 - 21

Week 4 – Days 22 – Month-end

TAURUS

TAURUS

Taurus Dates: April 20th to May 20th

Zodiac Symbol: Bull

Element: Earth

Planet: Venus

House: Second

Color: Green

Taurus is the second astrological sign in the zodiac, with birthdates spanning from April 20th to May 20th. This sign is pictured as the symbol of the bull and is associated with the Earth element, embodying qualities of stability, practicality, and a solid connection to the material world. Governed by the planet Venus, Taurus individuals possess an appreciation for beauty and luxury.

People born under the Taurus sign are patient, grounded in nature, and have a strong work ethic. They tend to take a steady and cautious approach to life, valuing security and stability. The bull symbolizes strength, determination, and reliability, reflecting key traits of Taurus individuals.

Taurus resides in the Second House of the zodiac and is closely linked to material possessions, personal values, and resources. This placement underscores Taurus' focus on the tangible aspects of life and their desire for stability and comfort.

The color green is commonly associated with Taurus due to its representation of growth, nature, and stability. This color aligns with Taurus' practical and down-to-earth qualities.

In summary, Taurus individuals exhibit patience, practicality, and a connection to the material world. Their dedication to stability, combined with their appreciation for beauty, makes them reliable and steadfast individuals.

The Chinese Zodiac is a system that assigns an animal sign to each year in a 12-year cycle, and each animal is associated with certain personality traits and characteristics.

The Year of the Snake, in particular, holds special significance within Chinese culture and is rich in symbolism.

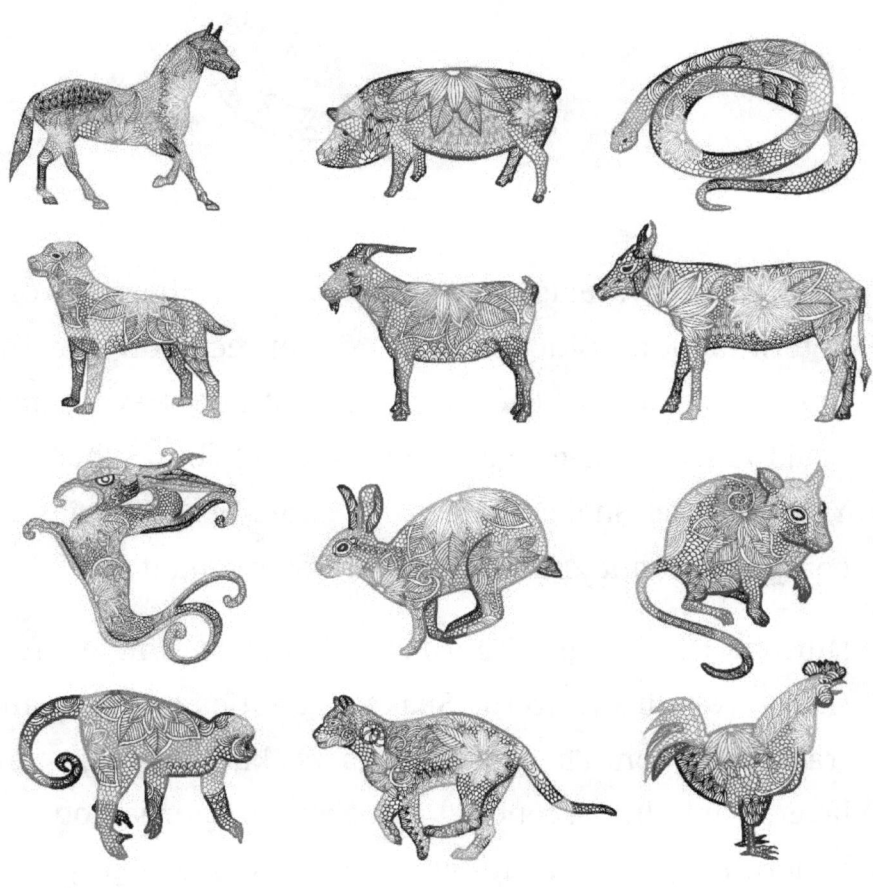

2025

The Chinese Year of the Snake

Taurus individuals are known for their strong determination, practicality, and appreciation for the finer things in life. They are steadfast in achieving their goals and are often grounded and reliable. When the Year of the Snake arrives, it combines energies to complement and enrich the Taurus personality.

During this year, Taurus individuals might find themselves drawn to the Snake's qualities of depth and transformation. The Snake sheds its skin to reveal a new layer, symbolizing renewal and growth. Taurus, too, can benefit from embracing this transformative energy.

The Year of the Snake encourages Taurus to explore their passions and interests more deeply. It's a time to dig beneath the surface and uncover hidden talents or potentials that often are overlooked. Taurus individuals might engage in self-improvement endeavors, whether pursuing a new hobby, developing a skill, or investing in personal well-being.

Taurus' appreciation for the tangible aspects of life can align well with the Snake's propensity for sensuality and aesthetic preference. This year might inspire Taurus to surround themselves with beauty and create harmonious environments that reflect their values.

In relationships, the Year of the Snake could prompt Taurus to explore the depths of emotional connections. Just as snakes navigate various environments with keen senses, Taurus might connect more deeply with their loved ones by genuinely understanding their feelings and needs.

While Taurus is known for practicality, the Year of the Snake invites them to embrace change and explore new horizons. It doesn't mean abandoning their grounded nature; it's about incorporating a sense of rejuvenation and exploration into their steady approach.

Ultimately, the Year of the Snake offers Taurus individuals an opportunity for personal growth and transformation. Taurus can find new ways to enhance their lives, pursue their passions, and build deeper connections with themselves and others by tapping into the Snake's symbolism of shedding the old and embracing the new.

TAURUS 2025
HOROSCOPE & ASTROLOGY

JANUARY WEEK ONE

Let's dive deeper into this cosmic journey! So, the Moon sliding into Capricorn is like your inner CEO taking the stage. You know, those days when you feel like a total boss and are ready to conquer the world? Yep, that's the Capricorn energy talking. It's all about your career, ambitions, and that drive to level up. You might even make ambitious to-do lists or have those late-night work marathons. It's that cosmic nudge to hustle harder but in a good way.

Here comes the main event - the New Moon. It's your moment to set some killer intentions, especially regarding your career goals and how you want to be seen. Maybe you're thinking about that promotion, launching a new project, or finally starting that side hustle you've been dreaming about. This New Moon is like a cosmic reset button, giving you a fresh start.

As the Moon slides into Aquarius, the universe hands you a sparkly neon sign that says, "Be Yourself, Unapologetically!" Aquarius is all about individuality and embracing your quirks. You feel the urge to break free from the norm and do things your way.

JANUARY WEEK ONE

☀ Brace yourself for a captivating wave of romantic and dreamy vibes as Venus gracefully waltzes into Pisces. This celestial move sprinkles a touch of enchantment over your love life and personal style, much like stardust falling from the heavens.

💧 Buckle up, for when Mars stands toe-to-toe with Pluto, it's a celestial battle royale filled with intensity and transformation. Your desires blaze like a bonfire, yet power struggles and buried motives may emerge from the shadows.

🌙 The Moon's graceful transition into Pisces bestows upon you a dreamy, intuitive aura that's akin to a celestial lullaby. It gently encourages introspection and invites a wander in the mystical realms of your soul.

☉ When the Sun forms a harmonious sextile with Saturn, it's akin to receiving a cosmic nod of approval for your unwavering commitment and hard work.

🌙 As the Moon charges boldly into Aries, imagine a surge of electrifying energy coursing through your veins. You're the cosmic trailblazer, primed for adventure.

JANUARY WEEK TWO

With Mercury's graceful entry into Capricorn, your thoughts turn practical and grounded. It's like a cosmic business meeting for your mind, urging you to plan and strategize with precision. Your communication takes on a more structured tone, and you're ready to tackle tasks.

As the Moon dances into Gemini, your curiosity and sociability soar. It's like a cosmic chat with your best friend, encouraging you to connect, communicate, and explore new ideas. Your mind is agile and adaptable, making it an ideal time for intellectual pursuits and light-hearted conversations.

Now, the Moon's tender transition into Cancer brings an emotional embrace. It's like a cosmic hug, inviting you to nurture your feelings and seek comfort in the familiar. Home and family take center stage, and you're drawn to create a cozy haven where your heart can flourish.

When Mars forms a harmonious trine with Neptune, it's a cosmic fusion of energy and dreams. This aspect fuels desires and empowers your artistic and spiritual pursuits, a cosmic muse whispering in your ear.

JANUARY WEEK TWO

☀ With the Sun forming a harmonious trine to Uranus, your individuality and innovation shine brightly. It's like a cosmic spotlight on your unique talents and ideas. You're ready to embrace change, break free from conventions, and ignite your inner revolutionary. Your creative spark is electrifying!

🌕 the Full Moon, a celestial climax! It's like the universe illuminating your path, revealing insights and revelations. Emotions run high, and you stand at the crossroads of completion and transformation. It's a cosmic call to release what no longer serves you and embrace the future with open arms.

🌙 As the Moon enters Leo, your inner performer takes center stage. It's like a cosmic Broadway show, encouraging you to shine, express, and dazzle the world.

✦ When Venus squares off with Jupiter, it's a cosmic debate between love and indulgence. You might feel torn between the desire for pleasure and the need for moderation. Balancing affections and cravings becomes a challenge. Sometimes, less is more in love matters.

JANUARY WEEK THREE

☼ When the Sun opposes Mars, it's like a cosmic war between your ego and desires. You may feel a push-pull between your assertive side and the need to channel your energy effectively. Finding a harmonious balance between action and patience is vital to navigating this celestial face-off.

☾ As the Moon gracefully moves into meticulous Virgo, you'll notice a shift towards practicality and a focus on the details. Your emotions align with your need for organization and efficiency, making it an ideal time to tackle tasks that require precision.

⚡ The Sun's sextile with Neptune adds a touch of enchantment to your life. You'll feel in sync with your dreams and intuition, allowing creative inspiration to flow effortlessly. The universe is giving you a gentle nudge to embrace your artistic side.

💜 Venus aligns with Saturn in a celestial embrace, bringing a sense of responsibility to your relationships and values. It's a cosmic reminder that enduring love and lasting partnerships require effort and dedication.

JANUARY WEEK THREE

🌙 As the Moon shifts into diplomatic Libra, you'll find yourself more attuned to harmony and balance in your interactions. This cosmic influence encourages you to seek fairness and compromise in your relationships.

☿ Mercury forms harmonious sextiles with Saturn and Venus, enhancing your communication skills and diplomacy. Your words carry weight and grace, making it a time for negotiations and heartfelt conversations.

♒ With the Sun's transition into Aquarius, you'll experience a shift towards innovation and a desire to connect with like-minded individuals. Your focus turns to community and humanitarian efforts, making it a great time to collaborate for a better future.

☀ The Sun's conjunction with Pluto ushers in transformation and empowerment. It's like a cosmic rebirth, allowing you to shed old layers and emerge as a more empowered version of yourself.

🌙 As the Moon enters the deep waters of Scorpio, emotions intensify, and you'll feel drawn to explore the hidden realms of your psyche.

JANUARY WEEK FOUR

🗣 Mercury's opposition to Mars sparks dynamic conversations and perhaps verbal fireworks. Your assertiveness is strong, but remember to avoid misunderstandings during this lively cosmic exchange.

⚡ Mercury's trine with Uranus electrifies your thoughts with unconventional brilliance. Your mind is a lightning bolt of inspiration, making it an ideal period for problem-solving and exploring inventive ideas.

🌙 As the Moon gracefully enters adventurous Sagittarius, you'll feel a call to expand your horizons. It's a time to seek knowledge, embrace new experiences, and explore uncharted territory.

💜 Venus forms a harmonious trine with Mars, igniting passion and desire in your relationships and creative pursuits.

🗣 Mercury's sextile with Neptune infuses your conversations with empathy and imagination.

🌙 Venus's sextile with Uranus ushers excitement and spontaneity in your relationships and finances. Be open to surprises in these areas.

JANUARY WEEK FOUR

Mercury's ingress into Aquarius marks a shift toward innovative and unconventional thinking. Your mind thrives on unique ideas and forward-thinking concepts.

As the Moon moves into quirky Aquarius, you'll feel a strong sense of individuality and a desire to connect with like-minded individuals who share your visionary ideas.

Mercury's conjunction with Pluto delves into the depths of your thoughts and conversations. It's a time of profound insights and transformative discussions.

The New Moon marks a fresh start and a time for setting intentions. You're planting the seeds for new beginnings and personal growth.

Uranus turns direct, releasing a surge of electrifying energy. It's a period of breakthroughs and sudden revelations, encouraging you to embrace change.

The Sun's trine with Jupiter brings a sense of expansion and optimism to your life. It's a time of growth, generosity, and opportunities for success.

FEBRUARY WEEK ONE

♥ When Venus dances in conjunction with Neptune, it's a cosmic ballet of romance and enchantment. Love takes on an ethereal, dreamlike quality during this celestial embrace, encouraging you to explore your deepest emotions and express your affections with poetic grace. It's a time to embrace the arts, allowing your heart to resonate with the world's beauty.

☾ As the Moon boldly charges into fiery Aries, your emotions catch fire with passion and determination. You'll feel a surge of energy as if the universe is urging you to seize the day and embark on new adventures. It's a cosmic call to action, prompting you to pursue goals.

💬 With Mercury forming a harmonious trine with expansive Jupiter, your communication takes on a broader, more optimistic tone. Your mind eagerly absorbs new knowledge, and conversations flow with wisdom and enthusiasm.

☾ The Moon's journey into sensual Taurus encourages your emotions to settle into grounded tranquility. You'll find solace in simple pleasures, seeking the familiar. This cosmic transition nurtures a connection to nature.

FEBRUARY WEEK ONE

🕊 As Venus gracefully steps into independent Aries, your love life and personal style receive an infusion of boldness and assertiveness. You'll take the lead in heart matters and confidently express your desires. It's a time to celebrate your individuality and take romantic risks.

⏩ Jupiter's direct motion signals a period of forward momentum and growth. Any projects or plans that may have been on hold can now progress with renewed vigor, and your sense of optimism expands. The universe encourages you to embrace new opportunities.

🌙 The Moon's transition into chatty Gemini sparks your social curiosity and intellectual thirst. Your communication skills shine brightly, and you'll relish connecting with a diverse range of people. It's a time for lively conversations and the exchange of ideas.

💜 Venus's harmonious sextile with transformative Pluto adds depth and intensity to your relationships and desires. This cosmic alignment invites you to explore the profound and passionate aspects of your connections. It's a time to delve into the mysteries of love and uncover hidden truths within your heart.

FEBRUARY WEEK TWO

☽ As the Moon gracefully glides into nurturing Cancer, your emotions take on a tender and compassionate tone. You'll find comfort in the familiarity of home and the warmth of family. It's a time when creating a cozy and secure environment becomes a priority.

☉ The Sun's conjunction with Mercury illuminates your mind with intellectual clarity and communicative prowess. Your thoughts and words align seamlessly, making it an excellent time for effective communication and mental clarity. It's like a celestial spotlight shining on your mental faculties.

♂ Mars forms a harmonious trine with Saturn, infusing your actions with discipline and strategic thinking. This cosmic alignment empowers you to tackle tasks with determination and lasting endurance. It's a period when your efforts are rewarded through patience and systematic progress.

☽ As the Moon enters lively Leo, your emotions are ignited with enthusiasm and a desire to shine. You'll seek opportunities for self-expression and creative outlets. It's a cosmic invitation to embrace individuality.

FEBRUARY WEEK TWO

⚡ The Sun squares off with Uranus, creating a cosmic tension that urges you to break free from routines and embrace change. While this aspect can bring surprises and disruptions, it's also an opportunity for liberation.

🌕 The Full Moon graces the night sky, marking a time of culmination and reflection. It's a moment to celebrate your achievements and consider the paths you wish to pursue. Emotions run high under the Moon's radiant glow.

🌙 The Moon's ingress into practical Virgo encourages attention to detail and a focus on practical matters. You'll find satisfaction in organization and productive tasks, making it an ideal time for tidying up loose ends.

💬 On Valentine's Day, Mercury transitions into dreamy Pisces, infusing your thoughts and communication with empathy and intuition. Your words take on a poetic and compassionate quality, making it an excellent time for heartfelt expressions of love and connection. This cosmic shift enhances your ability to tune into the emotions of others and engage in soulful conversations. It's a celestial gift for matters of the heart.

FEBRUARY WEEK THREE

🌙 With the Moon's graceful transition into harmonious Libra, the cosmos invites you to immerse yourself in the quest for equilibrium and beauty. Your emotions resonate with a longing for balance, from your relationships to your immediate surroundings. During this celestial phase, you'll find genuine joy in fostering peace and harmony in your interactions. It is an ideal time to mend any fractured connections and create an environment that exudes elegance and serenity.

🌙 As the Moon later delves into the enigmatic realms of Scorpio, the emotional landscape takes on a more profound and penetrating essence. Your feelings intensify, and you're naturally inclined to delve beneath the surface of life's experiences. It's as if a cosmic spotlight is cast upon your innermost desires and fears. This phase encourages emotional authenticity and a willingness to confront hidden aspects.

☉ The Sun's radiant ingress into Pisces signals a time of heightened sensitivity, artistic inspiration, and spiritual connection. You'll notice an increased awareness of the interconnectedness of all living things.

FEBRUARY WEEK THREE

When the Moon finds its way into adventurous Sagittarius, your spirits soar as you embark on a cosmic journey of optimism and exploration. It's as if the universe invites you to broaden your horizons, both mentally and physically. You'll be drawn to new experiences, philosophical insights, and a desire to learn and grow. This phase ignites your inner adventurer and encourages you to seek freedom and expansion in various aspects of your life.

Mercury's square with expansive Jupiter adds an intriguing twist to your communication style. While this aspect amplifies your enthusiasm and intellectual curiosity, it can lead to overly optimistic thinking. Your ideas may reach grand proportions, and you might be tempted to take on more than you can handle. During this cosmic encounter, balancing your visionary thinking with practicality is crucial. By channeling your expansive thoughts into actionable plans, you can harness the positive energy of this aspect for growth and progress.

FEBRUARY WEEK FOUR

🌙 As the Moon gracefully dips into steadfast Capricorn, your emotional landscape takes on a more grounded and pragmatic tone. You'll find yourself focused on responsibilities and long-term goals, making this an ideal time for planning and setting intentions for the future. Emotions may be expressed with determination and a desire for structure. During this lunar phase, you'll be drawn to activities that allow you to build a solid foundation for your dreams and aspirations.

🔴 Mars, the planet of action and drive, finally shifts into direct motion, bringing a surge of forward momentum to your endeavors. If you've felt like your energy has been in a holding pattern, prepare to feel a renewed sense of purpose and motivation. It's as if the cosmic traffic light has turned green, encouraging you to move confidently toward your goals with newfound vitality.

🌙 As the Moon transitions into open-minded Aquarius, your emotions take on an innovative and progressive quality. You'll be drawn to unconventional ideas, social causes, and intellectual pursuits. This lunar phase encourages you to embrace individuality and engage in humanitarian efforts.

FEBRUARY WEEK FOUR

☽ Mercury's conjunction with Saturn adds a touch of seriousness and structured thinking to your communication. Your words carry weight and gravitas during this cosmic alignment, making it an excellent time for careful planning, deep discussions, and long-term strategizing. This aspect encourages you to approach your intellectual pursuits with discipline.

☽ When the Moon moves into compassionate Pisces, your emotions flow with sensitivity and empathy. This lunar phase invites you to explore your inner world, dreams, and artistic inclinations.

☽ Mercury's sextile with Uranus sparks innovative thinking and exciting conversations. Your mind is open to unconventional ideas and unique solutions to challenges. This cosmic connection encourages you to embrace change and experiment with fresh perspectives. It's an excellent time for brainstorming, technological exploration, and connecting with visionary individuals who inspire your intellectual pursuits.

● The New Moon represents a decisive moment for setting intentions and initiating new beginnings.

MARCH WEEK ONE

☽ As the Moon confidently enters the fiery realm of Aries, your emotions ignite with a passionate and assertive energy. You'll strongly desire to take action, initiate new projects, and assert your individuality. It's a cosmic call to follow your instincts and embark on new adventures with courage and determination.

☽ Venus, the planet of love and beauty, begins its retrograde journey, inviting you to revisit matters of the heart and your values. Relationships and self-worth issues may come under the cosmic microscope during this introspective period. It's a time for reflection and reevaluation, allowing you to gain clarity about what truly matters in matters of love and personal values.

💬 Mercury's conjunction with Neptune adds a dreamy and imaginative quality to your thoughts and communication. Your mind is attuned to the mystical realms, making it an ideal time for creative and artistic endeavors. You may find inspiration in poetry, music, or spiritual pursuits; your intuition guides your conversations.

MARCH WEEK ONE

⚡ The Sun's square with expansive Jupiter brings optimism and enthusiasm to your life. While this aspect encourages you to dream big and aim high, it's essential to maintain a sense of balance and avoid overextending yourself. Be mindful of setting realistic goals and avoiding the temptation to take on too much. This cosmic influence encourages you to embrace growth.

🌙 Mercury's ingress into Aries marks a shift in your communication style. Your words become more direct and assertive, and you're unafraid to express your thoughts and ideas passionately. This cosmic transition encourages quick thinking and decisive communication.

🌙 The Moon's transition into sensual Taurus invites you to indulge in life's pleasures and prioritize comfort and stability. You'll find satisfaction in nurturing your senses and connecting with the physical world. It's a time when the simple joys of life take center stage.

💬 Mercury's sextile with Pluto adds depth and intensity to your conversations and mental pursuits. This cosmic connection encourages profound insights and transformative communication.

MARCH WEEK TWO

◯ The harmonious Sun trine Mars aspect infuses you with energy, motivation, and confidence. Your actions align effortlessly with your desires, making it an excellent time to pursue your goals and assert your individuality. You radiate strength and vitality, inspiring those around you with your enthusiasm.

🌙 As the Moon gracefully enters the regal sign of Leo, you'll feel a desire to shine and express your unique talents. Emotions take on a dramatic and playful flair; you'll be drawn to creative endeavors and activities that allow you to bask in the spotlight.

💬 Mercury's conjunction with Venus enhances your communication skills and social charm. Your words are imbued with grace and diplomacy, making it easy to connect with others on a deeper, more harmonious level.

🌙 The Moon's transition into pragmatic Virgo encourages practicality and attention to detail. You'll find satisfaction in getting organized, tackling tasks, and focusing on self-improvement. This lunar phase is ideal for refining your routines and addressing health and wellness matters.

MARCH WEEK TWO

◯ The Sun's conjunction with Saturn signifies a period of increased responsibility and a need for discipline. You may encounter challenges that require patience and perseverance. While this aspect may bring some obstacles, it also offers an opportunity to solidify long-term plans and commitments.

◯ The Full Moon illuminates your accomplishments and partnerships. It's a time to celebrate your achievements and evaluate your relationships, ensuring they align with your goals and aspirations. Emotions run high during this lunar climax, providing insights into areas needing adjustment.

⚡ The Sun's sextile with Uranus introduces innovation and excitement into your life. You're open to new ideas and experiences, making it a favorable time for exploring novel opportunities and embracing change.

☽ As the Moon moves into diplomatic Libra, you'll prioritize harmony and cooperation in your interactions. This lunar phase encourages you to cultivate partnerships that bring mutual satisfaction and equilibrium.

MARCH WEEK THREE

🔄 When Mercury turns retrograde, it's as if the cosmic messenger is taking a step back to review and reassess the flow of communication in your life. This period encourages you to reflect on your thoughts, ideas, and how you express yourself. Be prepared for potential miscommunications or delays, but embrace the opportunity to revisit past projects and reconnect with old acquaintances.

🌙 As the Moon delves into the intense and transformative sign of Scorpio, your emotions take on a deep and enigmatic quality. It's a time when you're drawn to explore the mysteries of life, both within yourself and in the world around you. Embrace this lunar phase as an opportunity for emotional regeneration and profound self-discovery.

🌙 As the Moon transitions into adventurous Sagittarius, a sense of optimism and wanderlust washes over you. This lunar phase encourages you to broaden your horizons, seek new experiences, and embrace the spirit of adventure. Your thirst for knowledge and exploration makes it ideal for travel and philosophical pursuits.

MARCH WEEK THREE

☉ When the Sun forms a conjunction with Neptune, the boundaries between reality and dreams blur, and your intuition is heightened. It's a mystical and imaginative period when your creativity and spirituality are heightened. Use this cosmic energy to tap into your artistic talents and engage in acts of compassion and empathy.

♈ As the Sun enters Aries, the zodiac's first sign, you enter the fiery realm of beginnings and fresh starts. Aries season marks the Vernal Equinox, a time of balance and equal daylight and nighttime hours. This cosmic shift infuses you with energy, courage, and a pioneering spirit. It's a time to initiate projects, assert individuality, and embrace opportunities for personal growth.

♇ The sextile between Venus and Pluto adds depth and intensity to your relationships and desires. It's as if your emotional connections take on a transformative and passionate quality. This cosmic alignment encourages you to explore your innermost desires and forge meaningful relationships based on authenticity and vulnerability. It's a time for profound emotional experiences and empowerment in matters of the heart.

MARCH WEEK FOUR

✦ The Sun's harmonious sextile with Pluto adds depth and intensity to your experiences. This cosmic connection sparks transformation and empowerment. The energy of this aspect empowers you to reshape your circumstances according to your true desires.

☾ As the Moon shifts into the intellectual and progressive sign of Aquarius, your emotional landscape opens up to innovative ideas and a sense of community. You'll feel drawn to unconventional thinking, group activities, and a desire to contribute positively to society. This lunar phase fosters a spirit of humanitarianism and encourages you to embrace your uniqueness.

☀ When the Sun aligns with Mercury, your mental faculties are razor-sharp, and your communication ability is enhanced. This celestial partnership supports precise, efficient, and persuasive conversations.

💬 Mercury's sextile with Pluto further deepens your communication prowess. Your words hold the potential to unearth hidden truths and stimulate transformative discussions. You may feel drawn to explore and research intriguing topics during this period.

MARCH WEEK FOUR

💜 The conjunction of Venus and Neptune amplifies the dreamy and romantic ambiance in your life. During this period, your creativity soars, and you may feel a strong desire to experience transcendent love and beauty. Your imagination knows no bounds, and you may find inspiration in artistic and spiritual pursuits.

🌝 As the Moon gracefully enters Aries, you'll experience energy and assertiveness. This cosmic call to action encourages you to take the lead, embrace challenges, and assert your desires with unwavering confidence. Initiating new endeavors and pursuing your goals with enthusiasm are favored during this lunar phase.

🌑 The arrival of the New Moon marks a fresh beginning and an opportunity to set new intentions. This lunar phase invites you to plant the seeds of your desires. It's a moment of renewal, offering you a cosmic blank canvas to paint your aspirations and embark on a journey of self-discovery.

🔱 With Neptune's entry into Aries, a new era of dreams and spiritual exploration dawns. This cosmic shift may inspire innovative and idealistic visions for the future.

APRIL WEEK ONE

🏠 The Moon's transition into Cancer shifts your focus to matters of home and family. Your emotions become centered on creating a cozy and nurturing environment. You may find solace in spending time with loved ones, tending to household tasks, or simply cherishing the comfort of your personal space.

♎ Saturn's sextile with Uranus brings a harmonious balance between tradition and innovation. This cosmic alignment invites you to embrace change while respecting the wisdom of established structures. It's a time when you can make practical and progressive strides in various areas of your life.

💧 Mars's sextile with Uranus ignites a spark of inspiration and bold action. You'll feel a surge of energy and a desire to break free from constraints, encouraging you to channel your enthusiasm into creative and innovative pursuits, fueling your ambitions.

� The trine between Mars and Saturn enhances your discipline and productivity. It's like a cosmic blueprint for achieving your goals through consistent effort and strategic planning.

APRIL WEEK ONE

☀ The Sun's sextile with Jupiter brings a sense of optimism and abundance. It's as though the universe is aligning in your favor, offering opportunities for growth and expansion. During this period, you'll find that your positive outlook and enthusiasm attract good fortune.

♥ Venus's trine with Mars sets the stage for harmonious interactions in love and desire. Your relationships are imbued with passion, cooperation, and a delightful synergy. It's a time when you can bridge the gap between your romantic desires and your ability to connect with others.

♣ The conjunction of Venus and Saturn adds a touch of seriousness and commitment to your relationships. You may find yourself evaluating your partnerships and making long-term plans. This alignment encourages you to build lasting foundations in matters of the heart.

☿ Mercury's direct motion signals a turning point in communication and decision-making. Clarity and forward momentum return as any previous misunderstandings or delays dissipate. It's a favorable time to move on projects and resolve lingering issues.

APRIL WEEK TWO

💕 Venus's sextile with Uranus sparks excitement and novelty in your relationships and pleasures. It's like a gentle cosmic breeze that carries unexpected delights and electrifying connections. During this time, you'll enjoy embracing change, exploring unique experiences, and expressing your individuality in matters of the heart. Expect pleasant surprises and a newfound sense of freedom in matters of the heart.

🌙 As the Moon gracefully transitions into Virgo, your emotions take on a practical and analytical hue. This lunar phase prompts you to focus on the finer points of life. This lunar phase encourages you to focus on the details, organize your thoughts, and focus on self-improvement. You may find solace in tackling tasks that require precision and order.

🌙 Moving into Libra, the Moon ushers in an atmosphere of harmony and diplomacy. During this lunar phase, your emotions are inclined towards seeking balance and fairness in your relationships. You'll find comfort in social interactions and may feel inspired to mend any emotional imbalances in your connections.

APRIL WEEK TWO

● The Full Moon is a pivotal moment in the lunar cycle, illuminating your path with its radiant light. It's a time of culmination and fruition, where the seeds you planted during the New Moon come to fruition. Emotions are heightened, and revelations may surface, guiding you toward necessary changes and closures. The Full Moon takes center stage, inviting you to reflect, release, and realign with your authentic path.

🔄 Venus's direct motion marks a significant shift in matters of love, beauty, and finances. After reflection and reevaluation, your love life and aesthetic pursuits start moving forward with newfound clarity. Relationships can regain harmony, and you'll feel more in sync with your desires. As Venus turns direct, the gentle tides of harmony and balance flow again, enriching your connections and experiences.

♏ As the Moon transitions into Scorpio, your emotions delve into intensity and transformation. It's a time when you're drawn to explore the hidden facets of your psyche and address emotional matters with depth and honesty. This lunar phase encourages introspection and rebirth.

APRIL WEEK THREE

💧 With Mercury's entrance into bold and fiery Aries, your communication style becomes assertive and direct. It's as if your words carry a spark of enthusiasm and courage. You're not afraid to speak your mind and take the initiative in conversations. This placement fosters a pioneering spirit in your thoughts and ideas, making it an excellent time to start new projects or share your innovative concepts with the world.

🌀 When Mercury aligns with dreamy Neptune, your mental landscape takes on a surreal and imaginative quality. It's like a cosmic poet's pen, allowing you to weave words and ideas into beautiful, ethereal tapestries. This aspect encourages creativity, intuition, and empathy in your communication. You may find yourself drawn to artistic or spiritual pursuits, using language to evoke emotions and inspire others.

🦁 Mars's ingress into bold and confident Leo infuses your actions with passion and a desire for recognition. You're unapologetically assertive about pursuing your wishes and goals. This placement encourages you to take center stage and express individuality with flair.

APRIL WEEK THREE

When Mars forms a harmonious trine with Neptune, your actions align with your dreams and ideals. It's like a cosmic current that carries your efforts toward compassionate and spiritually inspired goals. You may find that your actions have a subtle yet profound impact on the world.

Easter Sunday symbolizes rebirth and renewal, symbolizing the emergence of light and hope. It's a time for reflection, forgiveness, and celebrating new beginnings. Whether you observe this day for religious or cultural reasons, it reminds you of the transformative power of faith and love.

Venus Sextile Uranus celestial connection adds excitement and unpredictability to your relationships and social life. It's like a cosmic invitation to embrace change and novelty in matters of the heart. You may be drawn to unique individuals or experiences that challenge your routines. This aspect encourages you to celebrate your individuality and explore unconventional forms of love and connection.

APRIL WEEK FOUR

☾ As the Moon drifts into Pisces, your emotions become deep and dreamy, like a tranquil ocean. You may find yourself more intuitive and sensitive to the energies around you. It's a beautiful time for creative and spiritual pursuits, as your imagination is heightened.

� When the Sun forms a square with Pluto, it's as if the cosmos shines a spotlight on your inner transformations. This aspect can bring power struggles to the surface, urging you to confront control and authority issues. It's a time for empowerment, introspection, and releasing what no longer serves.

♣ Venus joining forces with Saturn brings a sense of commitment and responsibility to your relationships. You may feel a more profound need for stability and security in heart matters. This cosmic alliance encourages you to build lasting foundations in your romantic connections.

☐ With the Moon's shift into Aries, your emotions become more assertive and impulsive. It's like a cosmic call to action, inspiring progress. This lunar phase encourages independence and a pioneering spirit.

APRIL WEEK FOUR

🌱 As the Moon settles into Taurus, you'll find solace in the earthly pleasures of life. This lunar phase encourages you to savor the simple joys, from delicious meals to the beauty of nature. It's a grounding and stabilizing influence on your emotions.

🌑 The New Moon marks a fresh beginning, a chance to plant new seeds of intention. It's a time of setting goals and envisioning the future you desire. Use this lunar energy to start afresh in any area of your life where you seek growth and transformation.

💬 With the Moon's shift into communicative Gemini, your emotions take on a more intellectual and curious tone. You may find yourself eager to engage in lively conversations and gather information. It's a beautiful time for learning and socializing.

🚀 Venus entering Aries injects passion and spontaneity into your relationships and creative pursuits. You'll be more direct in matters of the heart and eager to express your desires. This transit encourages you to pursue what you want with confidence and enthusiasm.

MAY WEEK ONE

🏠 With the Moon entering Cancer, you're enveloped in a warm, nurturing emotional atmosphere. This lunar transit amplifies your connection to home and family, making it an ideal time for cozy gatherings and heart-to-heart conversations. Emotions run deep, and you find comfort in the familiar embrace of your domestic life.

🪐 The conjunction of Venus and Neptune creates an enchanting atmosphere in matters of the heart and aesthetics. It's like a romantic fairy tale weaves its way into your life. This aspect encourages you to appreciate the beauty in every corner of existence, fostering deep emotional connections and artistic inspiration. Love takes on a dreamy, ethereal quality, and creative pursuits flourish under the influence of this celestial union.

🔄 Pluto turning retrograde signifies a period of deep introspection and transformation. During this cosmic shift, you're encouraged to revisit and review the profound changes you've been undergoing. This retrograde period allows you to dig even deeper into the core of your desires and personal power.

MAY WEEK ONE

🩶 When Mercury forms a harmonious sextile with Jupiter, your thoughts are expansive, and your communication is optimistic. This celestial connection amplifies your ability to learn, share ideas, and engage in meaningful conversations. It's a time for open-mindedness, positivity, and the pursuit of knowledge.

🌙 As the Moon shifts into Virgo, your emotions become practical and analytical. You may find satisfaction in detailed tasks and efficient organization. This lunar phase encourages you to focus on self-improvement and engage in acts of service to others.

💘 Venus sextile Pluto brings intensity and depth to your relationships and creative pursuits. It's as if your heart beats in harmony with the profound mysteries of love and art. This aspect encourages transformative experiences in matters of the heart and exploring the hidden parts of your desires. Your connections become more meaningful, and you're drawn to artistic expressions that reflect the richness of life's complexities.

MAY WEEK TWO

☽ When the Moon gracefully moves into Libra, your emotions seek balance, harmony, and connection. Libra is the sign of partnerships and aesthetics, so you may find yourself drawn to activities that involve beauty, art, or social interactions. This lunar phase encourages you to seek compromise and cooperation and appreciate life's finer things.

☌ Mercury's ingress into Taurus brings a grounded and practical tone to your communication. Your words become steady and reliable, reflecting a desire for stability and tangible results. This planetary transit is an excellent time for discussing financial matters and indulging in discussions about the pleasures of life, such as good food and the arts.

♏ As the Moon delves into Scorpio, your emotions take on a deep and reflective quality. Scorpio's influence encourages you to explore your innermost feelings and the mysteries of life. This lunar phase promotes transformation, making it an excellent time for purging emotional baggage and embracing personal growth.

MAY WEEK TWO

The Full Moon is a culmination of energies when intentions set during the New Moon come to fruition. It's an influential period for completing projects, evaluating your goals, and reaping the rewards of your efforts. Emotions run high during a Full Moon, making it essential to find balance and release what no longer serves you.

Mercury's square with Pluto intensifies your mental processes, urging you to dive into the depths of your thoughts and perceptions. It's a time when you're compelled to uncover hidden truths and explore complex subjects. While this aspect can bring about power struggles in communication, it also offers the potential for profound insights and transformation.

As the Moon ventures into adventurous Sagittarius, your emotions are filled with enthusiasm and a thirst for knowledge. You're eager to expand your horizons through travel, education, or philosophical exploration. This lunar phase encourages you to embrace spontaneity and a sense of freedom, inspiring you to explore new frontiers.

MAY WEEK THREE

🔺 As the Moon gracefully enters Capricorn, your emotions take on a more pragmatic and disciplined tone. You're focused on your goals, responsibilities, and long-term plans. This lunar phase encourages you to approach your tasks with determination and purpose, making it an excellent time for productivity and achieving practical results.

⚡ The conjunction of the Sun and Uranus is a dynamic cosmic event that sparks innovation and unexpected developments. It's as if lightning strikes, awakening your desire for change and freedom. It encourages you to break free from routines and embrace your individuality, potentially leading to groundbreaking ideas and experiences.

💧 Mercury's square with Mars ignites your mental energy, making your thoughts and communication more assertive and direct. However, this aspect can also lead to impatience and impulsiveness in conversations. Choosing your words carefully and avoiding unnecessary conflicts during this time is essential.

MAY WEEK THREE

🏛 As the Moon enters Aquarius, your emotions take on an independent and forward-thinking vibe. You're drawn to unconventional ideas and group activities.

⏰ The Sun's sextile with Saturn brings a sense of discipline and structure to your endeavors. You're more willing to try to achieve your goals and take on responsibilities with a practical and systematic approach. This aspect fosters stability and the ability to make steady progress.

🌒 As the Moon moves into Pisces, your emotions take on a dreamy and compassionate quality. It's a time when you're more attuned to your intuition and the emotional needs of others. This lunar phase encourages creative and spiritual exploration and a deep connection to the mysteries of the universe.

☀ The Sun's ingress into Gemini marks a shift in focus towards communication, learning, and versatility. You become more curious, adaptable, and eager to engage in various activities. This solar transition encourages you to connect with others through conversation, expand your knowledge, and embrace the diversity of life.

MAY WEEK FOUR

☀ The Sun's sextile with Neptune brings a touch of magic to your life. You're more attuned to your dreams, intuition, and artistic sensibilities. This aspect encourages you to pursue creative and spiritual pursuits, as well as acts of compassion and empathy.

☄ The Sun's trine with Pluto marks a transformative and empowering celestial alignment. It's as if the cosmic forces support your personal growth and renewal. This aspect encourages you to embrace change, gain insights into your inner workings, and harness your inner power for positive transformation.

☿ Mercury's conjunction with Uranus sparks innovative thinking and lightning-fast insights. Your mind is buzzing with unique ideas and a thirst for knowledge. This cosmic aspect encourages change as you break from routine and explore groundbreaking concepts.

♄ Saturn's ingress into Aries marks a shift in your long-term goals and responsibilities. You're ready to take on new challenges and assert your individuality in pursuing your ambitions. This transit encourages you to develop self-confidence and maintain your authority.

MAY WEEK FOUR

📖 Mercury's sextile with Saturn brings a disciplined and focused approach to your thinking and communication. You're attentive to details and committed to your responsibilities. This aspect supports planning, organizing, and efficient problem-solving.

🌑 The New Moon marks a fresh beginning and an opportunity to set new intentions. It's like a cosmic reset button, allowing you to plant the seeds of your desires. This lunar phase encourages introspection and the formulation of new goals.

🔍 Mercury's trine with Pluto intensifies your thought processes and communication. You're drawn to profound conversations and keenly interested in uncovering hidden truths. This aspect encourages deep insights and transformation through words and ideas.

💬 The Sun's conjunction with Mercury brings a heightened focus on communication and self-expression. Your thoughts and ideas are illuminated, and you're more eager to engage in conversations and share your knowledge.

JUNE WEEK ONE

♍ When the Moon gracefully enters Virgo, your emotions adopt a practical and analytical tone. You're inclined to pay attention to the details and strive for perfection. This lunar phase encourages you to be of service, whether through acts of kindness or focusing on tasks that require precision and efficiency. It's a favorable time for organizing and tending to your well-being.

☽ As the Moon moves into Libra, your emotions take on a harmonious and friendly quality. You seek balance and harmony in your relationships, and you're more inclined to be a peacemaker. This lunar phase encourages cooperation, diplomacy, and a desire to connect with others on a deeper level.

✹ Venus sextile Jupiter brings a sense of joy and abundance to your relationships and personal values. You're open to new experiences, and your social interactions are characterized by optimism and a generous spirit. This aspect encourages you to enjoy the pleasures of life and expand your connections.

JUNE WEEK ONE

🚀 Mercury sextile Mars enhances your mental agility and communication. Your thoughts and ideas are assertive and directed toward action. This aspect fuels your enthusiasm, making it an excellent time for effective problem-solving and initiating conversations with confidence.

🌷 Venus's ingress into Taurus marks a shift toward a sensual and stable approach to love and values. You seek comfort and security in your relationships and surroundings. This transit encourages you to indulge in the sensory pleasures of life and cultivate a deeper appreciation for beauty.

♏ As the Moon moves into Scorpio, your emotions take on an intense and transformative quality. You're drawn to explore deeper emotional connections and may find yourself engaged in introspection. This lunar phase encourages you to release what no longer serves you and embrace your emotional authenticity. This lunar phase enables transformation and a desire to uncover hidden truths.

JUNE WEEK TWO

☀ Mercury's conjunction with Jupiter amplifies your mental faculties and brings an expansive and optimistic outlook. Your thinking becomes broad and visionary, and you may find yourself drawn to grand ideas and philosophical discussions. This aspect encourages learning and communication that inspires growth.

♋ Mercury's ingress into Cancer infuses your thinking with emotional depth and sensitivity. You become more in tune with your feelings in a nurturing and empathetic manner. This transit encourages discussions about family, home, and emotional security.

♄ Mercury's square with Saturn can add a touch of seriousness and responsibility to your communication. It's a time when you might encounter obstacles or delays in your plans, requiring patience and careful thought. This aspect encourages you to be precise and thorough in your conversations and commitments.

♐ As the Moon moves into Sagittarius, your emotions take on an adventurous and free-spirited quality. This lunar phase encourages you to seek knowledge, expand your horizons, and embrace a sense of optimism.

JUNE WEEK TWO

💔 Venus square Pluto brings intensity and power struggles to your relationships and desires. You may experience deep emotional transformations and a need to confront hidden issues. This aspect encourages you to examine the dynamics of your connections and make necessary changes.

🪴 Jupiter's ingress into Cancer marks a shift toward emotional growth and nurturing expansion. It's a time when you may find blessings and opportunities within your home and family life. Jupiter in Cancer encourages you to seek security, comfort, and a sense of belonging.

🌕 The Full Moon is a culmination of energy and a time to reap the rewards of your efforts. It's like a cosmic spotlight on your achievements and a chance to release what no longer serves you. This lunar phase encourages self-reflection and the fulfillment of goals.

💕 Mercury's sextile with Venus brings a harmonious and charming tone to your communication and relationships. It's a time when your words carry a touch of diplomacy and grace, making it easier to express your affection and appreciation.

JUNE WEEK THREE

⚡ Mars square Uranus brings a surge of rebellious and unpredictable energy. It's like a cosmic lightning bolt, stirring restlessness and a desire for change. This aspect can lead to impulsive actions, so caution is advised. Harness this energy for positive transformations and avoid unnecessary risks.

🏛 The Jupiter square Saturn aspect symbolizes a tug-of-war between expansion and restriction. While Jupiter seeks growth and optimism, Saturn imposes boundaries and discipline. This cosmic battle encourages you to find a balance between ambition and practicality, allowing for steady progress toward your goals.

☾ As the Moon enters Pisces, your emotions take on a dreamy and intuitive quality. This lunar phase encourages introspection, creative pursuits, and a connection to the mystical and emotional realms.

⛰ Mars's ingress into Virgo brings a shift in your actions and energy. You'll become more detail-oriented and focused on practical tasks. This transit encourages you to tackle projects with precision and efficiency. It's an excellent time for improving your daily routines.

JUNE WEEK THREE

💧 As the Moon enters Aries, your emotions become more assertive and dynamic. It's like a cosmic call to action, igniting your passion and drive. This lunar phase encourages you to embrace challenges with courage and take the lead in your endeavors.

🍷 Jupiter square Neptune stirs a sense of idealism and spiritual growth. It's like a cosmic tug towards the mystical and the transcendent. While this aspect can inspire creativity and a deepening of your beliefs, it also carries a risk of delusion. Find a balance between optimism and grounded discernment.

🌿 As the Moon moves into Taurus, your emotions take on a grounded and earthy quality. This lunar phase encourages you to connect with nature, enjoy delicious meals, and indulge in the simple joys of life.

🦀 The Sun's ingress into Cancer marks the June Solstice, a time when the Northern Hemisphere experiences the longest day of the year. Cancer season brings a focus on home, family, and emotional connections. It's a time to nurture and protect, creating a sense of emotional security.

JUNE WEEK FOUR

♎ When the Sun forms a square with Saturn, it's as if a cosmic reality check occurs. Responsibilities and limitations may come to the forefront, and you're asked to find the balance between your ambitions and the demands of the real world. This aspect encourages discipline and structure in your endeavors.

📖 Sun square Neptune can bring a sense of confusion and uncertainty. It's like a cosmic fog that obscures your clarity. During this aspect, you might grapple with illusions, miscommunications, or a lack of direction. It's vital to remain discerning and avoid hasty decisions.

☀ Sun conjunct Jupiter is a powerful and expansive aspect. It's like a cosmic blessing that amplifies your confidence and opportunities for growth. This aspect encourages you to think big, embrace your optimism, and have faith in your abilities. It's a time for abundance and good fortune.

🌑 The New Moon marks the beginning of a new lunar cycle. It's like a cosmic blank slate, inviting you to set intentions and start fresh in various areas. This lunar phase encourages introspection and evaluation.

JUNE WEEK FOUR

💧 Sun sextile Mars infuses your actions with dynamism and assertiveness. It's like a cosmic green light urging you to move forward with your plans and projects. This aspect encourages you to channel your energy constructively and take bold steps toward your goals.

💬 Mercury's move into Leo signifies a more expressive and creative mode of thinking. Your communication style becomes bolder, and you're eager to share your ideas with confidence. This transit encourages self-expression, storytelling, and a love for dramatic flair.

🏛 Mercury trine Saturn brings a sense of discipline and focus to your thoughts and communication. This aspect encourages you to follow through on commitments and approach tasks with a methodical mindset.

🔍 Mercury opposed Pluto can bring intensity and a desire for deep psychological understanding. It's like a cosmic detective, encouraging you to uncover hidden truths and explore the mysteries of the mind. This aspect may lead to deep, transformative conversations or encounters.

JULY WEEK ONE

🌙 When the Moon moves into Scorpio, your emotions take on an intense quality. This lunar phase encourages introspection, transformation, and a desire to explore what's hidden beneath the surface.

☾ Venus's conjunction with Uranus creates an electrifying and unpredictable energy in matters of love and beauty. It's like a cosmic bolt of excitement and change in your relationships and aesthetics. This aspect encourages you to embrace your uniqueness and be open to unconventional experiences.

▨ As Venus enters Gemini, your approach to love and social connections becomes more curious and communicative. Enjoy lively conversations and explore a variety of interests. This transit encourages intellectual stimulation and adaptability in your relationships.

🌀 Neptune turning retrograde signifies a period for internal reflection and spiritual contemplation. It's a retreat into the depths of your dreams and intuitions. This retrograde period encourages you to revisit your spiritual practices, connect with your inner self, and refine your artistic or creative visions.

JULY WEEK ONE

♎ Venus sextile Saturn brings stability and commitment to your relationships and artistic endeavors. It's like a cosmic contract of mutual respect and responsibility. This aspect encourages you to build lasting and meaningful connections while also honoring tradition and structure.

☾ Venus sextile Neptune adds a touch of magic and inspiration to your romantic and creative pursuits. It's like a cosmic brushstroke of ethereal beauty. This aspect encourages you to express your feelings through art and connect with others on a deep, soulful level.

⚡ Uranus's ingress into Gemini marks a period of intellectual excitement and innovation. It's like a cosmic awakening of your mental faculties and a desire for fresh ideas. This transit encourages you to embrace change in your thought patterns, communication style, and approach to learning.

✵ Venus trine Pluto deepens your connections and intensifies your desires. It's like a cosmic magnetism drawing you toward transformative experiences in love and creativity. This aspect encourages emotional depth.

JULY WEEK TWO

🌙 When the Moon gracefully moves into Capricorn, your emotions take on a more disciplined and responsible tone. It's like a cosmic mentor guiding your feelings, encouraging you to focus on your goals and long-term plans. This lunar phase promotes a structured and determined approach to your emotional world.

🌕 The Full Moon is a powerful climax in the lunar cycle, illuminating your achievements and bringing a sense of fulfillment. It's as if a cosmic spotlight shines on your emotions and projects, helping you see the results of your efforts. This phase encourages you to release what no longer serves you and acknowledge your accomplishments.

🌙 As the Moon shifts into Aquarius, an air of innovation and individuality permeates your emotional landscape. It's like a cosmic call to embrace your uniqueness and think outside the box. This lunar phase encourages you to connect with like-minded individuals and explore progressive ideas.

JULY WEEK TWO

⏪ Saturn turning retrograde initiates a period of reflection and review in matters of responsibility and structure. It's as if a cosmic teacher is asking you to revisit your commitments and long-term goals. This retrograde encourages you to fine-tune your plans, reassess your limitations, and learn valuable lessons from the past.

☾ When the Moon moves into Pisces, your emotions take on a dreamy and intuitive quality. It's like a cosmic lullaby, encouraging introspection and a connection to the mystical realms. This lunar phase invites you to explore your inner world, pay attention to your dreams, and engage in acts of compassion and creativity.

This week, the celestial transitions guide you through a range of emotional experiences, from discipline and accomplishment to innovation and introspection. Each phase offers unique opportunities for growth and self-discovery, allowing you to align your emotions with your long-term goals and personal evolution.

JULY WEEK THREE

🌙 When the Moon gracefully enters Aries, your emotional world is set ablaze with a surge of dynamic energy. It's as if a cosmic trumpet sounds, beckoning you to seize the day and lead with courage. During this lunar phase, you're encouraged to embrace your adventurous spirit and approach life with unbridled enthusiasm.

🔄 Mercury's retrograde journey marks a period of deep introspection and recalibration in the domain of communication and thought. During this celestial event, your mental processes slow down, allowing you to reflect on your ideas, past conversations, and the way you connect with others. It's a cosmic call to tidy up misunderstandings, clarify thoughts, and fine-tune the intricate instrument of your thinking.

🌙 As the Moon gracefully glides into Taurus, a soothing sense of stability and grounding envelops your emotional realm. During this lunar placement, you're encouraged to indulge in life's simple pleasures, connect with the natural world, and savor the sensory experiences that bring tranquility to your soul.

JULY WEEK THREE

💚 The harmonious alignment of Mercury sextile Venus creates a celestial bridge between your mind and heart. It's as if your thoughts and feelings engage in a melodic waltz, perfectly synchronized. This aspect paves the way for sweet, meaningful communication. You'll find that your conversations are imbued with affection, making it an ideal time to express your love and appreciation.

🌙 With the Moon's ingress into Gemini, your emotional landscape takes on a curious and communicative aura. It's like a cosmic storyteller awakens within you, eager to share your feelings and ideas with the world. During this lunar phase, intellectual curiosity is at its peak.

In this multifaceted cosmic dance this week, you are invited to explore a rich tapestry of emotions and experiences. From the spirited fire of Aries to the reflective pause of Mercury retrograde, the grounding embrace of Taurus, the harmonious blending of mind and heart, and the communicative spirit of Gemini, each phase offers a unique opportunity for self-discovery and connection with the world around you. Embrace these celestial energies as they guide you on a journey of exploration and growth.

JULY WEEK FOUR

🏛 When the Sun forms a harmonious sextile with Uranus, the universe is sending a lightning bolt of inspiration your way. This cosmic alignment encourages you to break free from routines and explore innovative ideas and opportunities. You're primed for creative, out-of-the-box thinking and a desire to embrace change and unconventional approaches. This aspect fuels your spirit of independence and sparks your inner genius.

💔 Venus square Mars creates a celestial tension in matters of love and desire. It's like a cosmic tug-of-war between the goddess of love and the warrior of passion. This aspect can stir up romantic conflicts and passionate disputes, highlighting the differences between what you want and what you need in relationships. While this may introduce challenges, it's also an opportunity for growth and understanding, encouraging you to balance your desires with consideration for others.

🏛 When the Sun forms a trine with Saturn, it's akin to a cosmic pat on the back for your hard work and dedication. This harmonious aspect brings a sense of stability and accomplishment to your endeavors. You'll find that your discipline and focus pay off.

JULY WEEK FOUR

🌑 The arrival of the New Moon symbolizes fresh beginnings and new possibilities. It's like a cosmic reset button, allowing you to set new intentions and embark on a journey of self-discovery. This lunar phase encourages you to plant the seeds of your desires, nurturing them with hope and determination. It's a time for introspection and envisioning the future you wish.

🏠 Venus' ingress into Cancer infuses your relationships and desires with a sense of nurturing and emotional connection. It's like a cosmic embrace from the goddess of love, encouraging you to seek comfort and security in your relationships with others. During this transit, you'll find that you're drawn to creating a warm and supportive atmosphere in your romantic life.

💧 As the Sun aligns with Mercury, it's like a cosmic conversation between your core identity and your intellect. This conjunction enhances your ability to express yourself with clarity and conviction. Your mind is sharp, and you're eager to communicate your thoughts and ideas. This aspect fuels your desire for self-expression and intellectual exploration.

AUGUST WEEK ONE

💔 Venus square Saturn sets the stage for a cosmic showdown between the planet of love and the stern taskmaster of the zodiac. It's as if you're caught in a complex web of emotions and responsibilities. In matters of the heart, this aspect can bring about a deep sense of longing and desire for closeness, but at the same time, it triggers a need for structure and boundaries. You might find yourself grappling with the age-old dilemma of love versus duty. It's crucial to strike a balance between your romantic aspirations and your commitments so both can coexist harmoniously.

🌙 Venus square Neptune adds an ethereal and somewhat confusing layer to your emotional landscape. This aspect is like wading through a sea of dreams and illusions, where reality blurs at the edges. In the realm of love and relationships, it can lead to misunderstandings or idealizing someone beyond what's realistic. Your heart may yearn for the romantic and poetic, but it's essential to keep your feet firmly on the ground. Trust your intuition, but ensure that your emotions remain grounded in truth.

AUGUST WEEK ONE

♐ The Moon's ingress into Sagittarius sets your emotional compass on a course of adventure and exploration. You'll feel a surge of enthusiasm and a desire to broaden your horizons. During this lunar phase, you're drawn to learning and personal growth. It's the perfect time to embark on a journey, either metaphorically or literally, that feeds your curiosity and expands your worldview.

♑ As the Moon shifts into Capricorn, a more pragmatic and grounded emotional energy takes hold. Under this influence, you may find satisfaction in taking charge of your duties and making tangible progress, especially in your professional life. Your emotions align with your ambitions, and you'll be willing to put in the hard work needed to achieve your objectives.

♎ Mars's ingress into Libra introduces a sense of equilibrium and diplomacy into your actions. This cosmic shift encourages you to approach conflicts and challenges with a sense of grace and cooperation. Instead of bulldozing your way through, you'll be more inclined to seek common ground and find peaceful resolutions.

AUGUST WEEK TWO

🚀 When Mars forms a trine with Uranus, it's like the cosmos hands you a rocket and says, "Blast off into the unknown!" This dynamic aspect ignites your inner fire and gives you the courage to break free from routine and convention. You're ready to embrace change, take risks, and explore new horizons. This energy can lead to exciting breakthroughs and unexpected opportunities. The key is to channel this fiery force constructively and avoid impulsive actions. By doing so, you can achieve remarkable progress and innovation.

🌒 The Full Moon marks a significant moment of culmination and revelation in the lunar cycle. It's a time when the Sun, representing your conscious self, opposes the Moon, symbolizing your emotions and instincts. This cosmic opposition often brings matters to a head and illuminates hidden truths. You may experience a heightened sense of awareness and strong emotions during this phase. It's an excellent time for releasing what no longer serves you and finding clarity in your life's direction.

AUGUST WEEK TWO

♋ As Mercury turns direct, the cosmic gears shift from reverse to forward. It's like the roadblocks and miscommunications that may have plagued the retrograde period are now cleared. With Mercury moving in the right direction, you'll find it easier to express yourself, make decisions, and communicate effectively.

♎ Saturn sextile Uranus brings a harmonious blend of tradition and innovation to the cosmic table. It's as if the old guard and the avant-garde find common ground. This aspect allows you to embrace change and progress without completely discarding what's tried and true. It's a time when you can create new structures, systems, or approaches that honor both the past and the future. This harmonious cooperation between Saturn and Uranus encourages you to find creative solutions and make lasting improvements.

♌ When Venus conjuncts Jupiter, it's like the cosmic sweethearts unite for a celestial celebration of love and abundance. Your heart is open, and you're more inclined to experience harmonious relationships and pleasures. Under this influence, opportunities for love, financial growth, and personal fulfillment abound.

AUGUST WEEK THREE

✦ When Mercury forms a harmonious sextile with Mars, it's akin to having a powerful mental engine at your disposal. Your thoughts are agile, and your ability to convey them is fueled by confidence and enthusiasm. This aspect is a cosmic green light for effective communication, making it an excellent time for crucial discussions, strategic planning, or pursuing tasks that require both mental precision and a touch of boldness.

☽ As the Moon gracefully glides into the versatile sign of Gemini, your intellectual curiosity is awakened. This lunar shift encourages you to explore new ideas, engage in stimulating conversations, and absorb information like a sponge. It's a perfect time for learning, networking, or simply enjoying the diversity of thought that surrounds you.

✦ The recurrence of Mercury's sextile to Mars further amplifies your mental prowess and assertiveness. Your words become your allies, allowing you to express your thoughts with eloquence and confidence. This aspect is a celestial nod to problem-solving so you can tackle those challenging issues that have been on your mind.

AUGUST WEEK THREE

🌙 When the Moon transitions into the tender sign of Cancer, emotions take center stage. You'll likely find yourself more in tune with your feelings and those of your loved ones. This lunar energy makes it an ideal time to connect with family and close friends. This lunar placement establishes an atmosphere of emotional nurturing, making it an excellent time for deepening connections with loved ones and finding comfort in the familiarity of home.

✺ The Moon's journey through Leo adds a touch of theatrical flair to the cosmic play. You might feel a magnetic pull toward self-expression, creativity, and sharing your unique talents with the world. This lunar influence encourages you to embrace your inner child, indulge in hobbies that bring you joy, and celebrate your individuality. It's a reminder to let your light shine brightly, for the world is your stage, and you are the star of your show. This lunar influence encourages you to embrace your inner artist, share your unique talents, and bask in the limelight. It's a time for infusing joy into your pursuits and letting your inner child come out to play.

AUGUST WEEK FOUR

☺ As the Sun gracefully moves into meticulous Virgo, it heralds a season of practicality, attention to detail, and a focus on organization. You may find yourself drawn to tasks that require precision and efficiency, making it an excellent time to tackle projects that demand careful planning and methodical execution. The Virgo influence encourages self-improvement and a commitment to health and well-being.

🌑 The New Moon marks a fresh beginning, a clean slate in the lunar calendar. It's a potent time to set intentions, start new ventures, or initiate changes in your life. During this lunar phase, you're planting the seeds for future growth and manifestation. Take a moment to reflect on your goals and aspirations as the universe aligns to support your new beginnings.

⚡ When the Sun forms a challenging square with Uranus, it's as if a bolt of cosmic electricity jolts you out of your comfort zone. This aspect encourages you to embrace change and innovation. Be open to unexpected developments and be willing to adapt to new circumstances. While it can be unsettling, this energy can lead to breakthroughs and liberation from old patterns.

AUGUST WEEK FOUR

◐ Venus' harmonious trine with Saturn brings stability and commitment to your relationships. This aspect encourages long-lasting connections, reliability, and a sense of responsibility in matters of the heart. It's an ideal time to strengthen bonds and make commitments.

✦ Venus' sextile with Uranus adds a touch of excitement and spontaneity to your interactions. Be open to novel experiences, unconventional relationships, and a spirit of adventure in love. This energy sparks creativity and innovation in your connections with others.

💧 Venus' trine with Neptune enhances the romantic and dreamy atmosphere. It fosters deep emotional connections, compassion, and a sense of soulful love. You may find yourself more attuned to the subtler, more spiritual aspects of your relationships.

🍃 Uranus' sextile with Neptune combines innovation with spirituality. It fosters a sense of higher purpose and the possibility for transformative insights. This aspect encourages you to seek out new and unconventional spiritual paths and transcend boundaries.

SEPTEMBER WEEK ONE

🍃 Saturn's entrance into Pisces marks a period of spiritual reflection and emotional depth. You'll find yourself more attuned to your inner world and may seek a deeper understanding of your emotions. This transit encourages you to embrace empathy, intuition, and compassion. It's a time to revisit your dreams and aspirations, allowing your imagination to guide you toward a more profound sense of purpose.

📁 Mercury's move into Virgo sharpens your analytical skills and attention to detail. This transit supports your practical thinking and problem-solving abilities. You'll excel in tasks that require precision and organization. It's an excellent time for getting your life in order and focusing on health and wellness.

⚡ When Mercury squares Uranus, you'll experience a burst of mental energy and potentially unexpected insights. This aspect encourages innovative thinking, but it can also make your mind a bit restless. Be open to new ideas and flexibility in your thought processes. It's a time for breaking free from mental routines and embracing change.

SEPTEMBER WEEK ONE

☄ The Mars Jupiter square ignites a desire for expansion and adventure. You'll have plenty of energy to tackle your goals and ambitions, but be mindful not to overextend yourself. This aspect can lead to taking on too much, so remember to pace yourself. If you channel this energy wisely, it can lead to impressive achievements.

🔄 Uranus turning retrograde signals a period for internal exploration. During this time, you'll review the changes and innovations you've experienced over the last few months. It's a phase for integrating new insights and finding more profound meaning in your life. Look inward to discover your unique path to personal liberation.

🌝 The Full Moon is a culmination of energy and a time to reap the rewards of your efforts. It's an excellent moment to reflect on your goals and intentions set during the previous New Moon. Emotions may run high during this phase, so use this time for self-awareness and introspection.

SEPTEMBER WEEK TWO

🌙 As the Moon gracefully transitions into Aries, it ignites a spark of enthusiasm within your emotional landscape. You'll find yourself invigorated, ready to tackle challenges head-on, and inclined to take the lead in your endeavors. This surge of energy can be a powerful motivator to start new projects, assert your individuality, and fearlessly embark on adventures.

🌙 When the Moon then moves into Taurus, a noticeable shift occurs, grounding your emotions in a practical and stable realm. During this phase, you seek comfort, security, and the finer things in life. It's an ideal time to indulge in life's sensual pleasures, pamper yourself, and pay closer attention to financial matters. This lunar influence encourages you to create a sense of security.

☀ The Sun's harmonious sextile with expansive Jupiter ushers in a wave of optimism and opportunities. This celestial pairing acts as a cosmic pat on the back, boosting your self-assurance and encouraging you to aim high. You're naturally inclined to broaden your horizons, both in thought and action. It is an auspicious time to set ambitious goals, explore new avenues, and embrace experiences that expand your worldview.

SEPTEMBER WEEK TWO

☽ With the Moon entering communicative Gemini, your curiosity takes center stage. You become more friendly and adaptable, seeking intellectual stimulation and the company of others. It's a favorable period for networking, engaging in lively conversations, and exploring a variety of interests.

✹ Mercury's harmonious sextile with Jupiter elevates your communication skills and intellectual prowess. This alignment fosters clarity of thought and the ability to articulate your ideas with finesse. It's a brilliant phase for planning, studying, and sharing your insights with a broader audience. Your optimism and enthusiasm are in sync with your intellectual pursuits, making it a suitable time for success in academic and creative ventures.

◯ The conjunction of the Sun and Mercury brings your thoughts and self-expression into perfect alignment. During this period, you'll experience mental clarity and a heightened ability to articulate your ideas effectively. Your words carry weight, and your decisions are made with confidence. This alignment offers a fantastic opportunity for meaningful conversations and successful communication.

SEPTEMBER WEEK THREE

💚 The alignment of Venus and Mars in a harmonious sextile creates a passionate and romantic atmosphere. Your relationships are imbued with a sense of balance and cooperation, allowing you to express your desires and affections with grace and charm. This cosmic connection enhances your love life, making it an excellent time for romantic endeavors and shared pleasures.

💬 However, the opposition between Mercury and Saturn may present communication challenges. Conversations could be more serious-minded and burdened by responsibilities, requiring patience and precision. While you may face obstacles in conveying your thoughts, the perseverance to overcome them can lead to valuable insights.

✳ Mercury's entrance into diplomatic Libra further enhances your communication style, promoting fairness, cooperation, and diplomacy in your interactions. You find it easier to seek compromise and harmony in your conversations, making it a favorable time for resolving disputes and fostering understanding.

SEPTEMBER WEEK THREE

🪐 Mercury's trine aspects with both Uranus and Pluto infuse your mind with intellectual brilliance and transformative insights. These cosmic connections encourage innovation and adaptability, empowering you to embrace unconventional ideas and break free from the constraints of tradition.

❀ As Venus enters practical Virgo, a more analytical and systematic approach to love and relationships prevails. You derive pleasure from tending to the finer details of your romantic connections, making this an ideal time for improvements and refinements in your love life.

☀ The Sun's opposition with responsible Saturn may present obstacles in self-expression and personal authority. Patience and determination are vital to overcoming these challenges, as they may serve as valuable lessons in personal growth and perseverance.

🌑 With the arrival of a New Moon, a fresh chapter begins, offering the opportunity to set new intentions and embark on a journey of self-discovery and personal development.

SEPTEMBER WEEK FOUR

💧 Mars' transition into Scorpio marks a period of intensified passion and determination. You're ready to take on challenges with unwavering resolve. Your desires run deep, and you'll stop at nothing to achieve your goals. This cosmic influence ignites a powerful inner fire that fuels your ambitions.

☀ The September Equinox, a celestial event marking the changing of seasons, carries a profound message of balance and adaptation. Much like the natural world adjusts to the shifting seasons, you're reminded to find equilibrium in your life. It's a reasonable time for reflection, self-assessment, and realigning your goals with the changing circumstances.

♎ As the Sun graces Libra, your focus turns toward relationships and partnerships. Your innate desire for harmony and fairness in your interactions shines brightly. It's a phase that encourages you to address any imbalances in your personal and professional connections, fostering a sense of equilibrium and mutual understanding.

SEPTEMBER WEEK FOUR

⚡ The Sun's harmonious trines with Uranus and Pluto infuse your life with a potent mix of transformation and innovation. You become more open to change and eager to embrace new ideas and experiences. This period prompts personal growth, making you adaptable and resilient in the face of challenges.

☽ As the Moon transitions into Scorpio, it ushers in a period of introspection and self-discovery. Your emotions delve into the depths of your psyche, compelling you to understand your motivations and desires on a profound level. It's a time for unraveling the mysteries within.

🏺 Nevertheless, the square between Mars and Pluto carries the potential for power struggles and conflicts. To navigate this aspect successfully, employ diplomacy and tact. Avoid provoking confrontations, and instead, seek common ground and compromise.

🏔 The Moon's subsequent shift into Sagittarius infuses your emotions with a spirit of adventure and expansion. You become open to new horizons, both in your intellectual pursuits and emotional experiences.

OCTOBER WEEK ONE

🌙 When the Moon moves into Aquarius, you may feel a sense of liberation and a desire to break free from the ordinary. Your mind is open to unconventional ideas and humanitarian causes, making this a great time to engage with your community and explore your intellectual pursuits.

🜛 A square between Mercury and Jupiter, however, can create a clash between details and big-picture thinking. While you may be enthusiastic about your ideas, it's essential to ensure that your plans are grounded in practicality. Find a balance between your optimism and the specifics of your projects.

🌒 As the Moon enters Pisces, your emotions take on a dreamy and compassionate quality. You're more attuned to the needs of others, making this an excellent time for acts of kindness and empathy. Dive into creative or spiritual activities to explore your inner world.

🚀 With the Moon's entry into Aries, your energy surges, and you're ready for action. t is a dynamic time for pursuing personal goals and passions. Your assertiveness and courage propel you forward.

OCTOBER WEEK ONE

🕵 Mercury's move into Scorpio adds depth and intensity to your thinking. You're inclined to investigate matters thoroughly and may become more interested in uncovering hidden truths. This cosmic transit is a period for deep introspection and a desire to get to the bottom of complex issues.

🌕 The Full Moon casts its radiant glow, illuminating your path. It's a time of culmination and realization. Reflect on your intentions set during the New Moon and see how they've developed. It is an opportunity to release what no longer serves you and move forward with clarity.

🪨 However, a square between Mercury and Pluto intensifies your communication and thought processes. While you're determined and focused, be cautious of becoming obsessed with ideas or engaging in power struggles. Maintain an open dialogue and avoid fixating on specific outcomes. The Mercury-Pluto square intensifies your communication but requires balance. Embrace the ebb and flow of these celestial tides, finding harmony between your intellectual and emotional worlds. 🌙 🚀 🌎 🌕 ✨

OCTOBER WEEK TWO

🌙 As the Moon gracefully enters Taurus, you find yourself in a tranquil cosmic embrace. This celestial shift invites you to slow down, appreciate the tangible beauty around you, and savor the sensory delights of the earthly realm. Taurus, an earth sign ruled by Venus, encourages you to connect with nature, indulge in self-care, and revel in the pleasures that bring comfort to your soul.

⭐ The harmonious sextile between Venus, the planet of love and beauty, and expansive Jupiter paints your social interactions with a palette of warmth and generosity. It's a celestial invitation to expand your connections, enjoy the company of others, and share moments of joy and abundance. This alignment encourages you to appreciate the finer things and cultivate a spirit of benevolence.

◐ Venus, now gracing Libra, engages in a celestial dance of opposition with the stern and structured Saturn. This cosmic interplay introduces a nuanced tension into matters of love and aesthetics. Finding the balance between your desires and practical considerations becomes paramount. Approach relationships and artistic pursuits with patience and a diplomatic touch.

OCTOBER WEEK TWO

💚 Venus, now in Libra, adds an elegant touch to your interactions, but an opposition with dreamy Neptune introduces an element of ambiguity.

🔄 Pluto's direct motion signals a profound shift in the cosmic energies. It's as if the universe is whispering, urging you to embrace transformation and release any lingering shadows. This period becomes a powerful portal for inner growth and shedding what no longer serves your highest good.

☀ The Moon's entrance into Leo infuses the cosmic canvas with a radiant and theatrical energy. Now is the time to express your authentic self, stepping into the spotlight with creativity and self-assurance.

☾ Venus, in a harmonious trine with innovative Uranus, injects excitement into your love life and creative endeavors. Embrace spontaneity and be open to unconventional expressions of affection. This alignment sparks a delightful unpredictability and originality.

🌀 Venus's trine with Pluto adds depth and intensity to your connections. This cosmic dance encourages transformative experiences in matters of the heart.

OCTOBER WEEK THREE

☽ As the Moon gracefully steps into meticulous Virgo, the cosmic energy shifts towards a focus on details and practicalities. Your emotional landscape aligns with a desire for order and efficiency, prompting you to find satisfaction in the small, everyday accomplishments that contribute to a sense of well-being.

☉ The square between the radiant Sun and expansive Jupiter hints at a cosmic tension between confidence and the need for moderation. While Jupiter encourages grand visions and optimism, the Sun's square prompts a reality check. It's a celestial reminder to balance your aspirations with a grounded approach, ensuring that your journey is both ambitious and sustainable.

☽ Transitioning into Libra, the Moon invites you into a harmonious dance of relationships and connections. The cosmic energies nudge you to seek balance in your interactions, fostering a sense of fairness and understanding. This phase encourages you to appreciate the beauty of harmonious connections and to find equilibrium in your emotional exchanges.

OCTOBER WEEK THREE

◯ Mercury's conjunction with assertive Mars adds a spark to your communicative style. Thoughts and words align with dynamic action, empowering you to express yourself with clarity and assertiveness. This cosmic duo fuels mental understanding and strategic thinking, propelling you toward effective decision-making.

● The New Moon marks a potent moment of cosmic reset, inviting you to set new intentions and embark on a fresh chapter. In the transformative sign of Scorpio, this lunar phase encourages introspection and the release of old patterns. Embrace the energy of rebirth and envision the path ahead with a spirit of renewal.

♏ As the Moon gracefully glides into Scorpio, the cosmic currents deepen, urging you to explore the mysteries of your emotions and subconscious. It's a time for embracing transformation and delving into the layers of your psyche, allowing hidden truths to surface.

In this cosmic journey, the Moon's transitions guide you through practicality, relationship harmony, and transformative introspection. The New Moon in Scorpio opens a portal to renewal and fresh beginnings. ☽ ● ♏

OCTOBER WEEK FOUR

○ As the Sun gracefully steps into Scorpio, the cosmic spotlight turns toward themes of transformation, regeneration, and the exploration of more profound truths. This solar journey encourages you to embrace the shadows, fostering a process of empowerment.

● The square between the potent Sun and transformative Pluto brings a celestial challenge, compelling you to confront power dynamics and hidden truths. This cosmic dance invites you to navigate the depths of your psyche, releasing that which no longer serves your growth.

☿ Mercury's harmonious trines with expansive Jupiter and structured Saturn create a cosmic bridge between intellect and wisdom. This alignment enhances your mental acuity, fostering a balance between visionary thinking and practical considerations. It's a favorable time for learning, communication, and strategic planning.

♂ Mars' trine with Jupiter ignites a spark of enthusiasm and courage. This cosmic alliance empowers your actions with a sense of purpose and confidence.

OCTOBER WEEK FOUR

☾ Mercury's trine with Neptune adds a touch of inspiration to your thoughts and communications. This ethereal connection enhances your creativity and intuition, allowing you to express yourself with a poetic and imaginative flair.

♐ As Mercury enters Sagittarius, the cosmic narrative takes on an adventurous tone. This transit encourages expansive thinking, a thirst for knowledge, and a willingness to explore new horizons. Embrace the spirit of exploration in your mental pursuits.

♂ Mars' trine with Saturn brings a harmonious alliance between action and discipline. This cosmic collaboration empowers you to pursue your goals with a structured and strategic approach, ensuring long-lasting and meaningful results.

⚡ Mercury's opposition to Uranus adds a touch of unpredictability to your thoughts and communications. Expect the unexpected in your mental landscape, and be open to innovative ideas and perspectives that challenge the status quo.

NOVEMBER WEEK ONE

♎ Venus squares Jupiter, creating a celestial dance between the planet of love and beauty and the expansive energy of Jupiter. While this alignment can bring a sense of abundance and optimism to relationships, be mindful of excesses. Balance your desires with realistic expectations, avoiding overindulgence.

♐ Mars forms a harmonious trine with Neptune, blending the assertive energy of Mars with the dreamy and imaginative influence of Neptune. This cosmic alliance encourages you to pursue your goals with creativity and sensitivity. Trust your intuition and allow your actions to be guided by a higher vision.

♂ Mars' ingress into Sagittarius injects enthusiasm and a sense of adventure into your pursuits. This cosmic alignment ignites the fire within, inspiring you to explore new territories and broaden your horizons. Embrace a spirit of exploration as you navigate the journey ahead.

☾ As the Moon enters Taurus, a stabilizing influence descends, grounding the fiery energies with a touch of earthiness. This lunar transit invites you to connect with the sensual and material aspects of your existence.

NOVEMBER WEEK ONE

⚡ Mars opposes Uranus, creating a dynamic and potentially volatile energy. This aspect encourages you to break free from constraints, but it's essential to channel this rebellious energy mindfully. Be open to change, but avoid impulsive actions that may lead to unnecessary disruptions.

🌕 The Full Moon illuminates the skies, casting its radiant light on your achievements and illuminating any areas of your life that may need balance. Take a moment to reflect on your goals, and adjust course if necessary.

💪 Mars sextile Pluto empowers your actions with a transformative force. This celestial alliance supports strategic and focused efforts, allowing you to overcome obstacles and make significant progress toward your objectives. Dive deep into your passions and harness the potency of this cosmic collaboration.

🌹 Venus' ingress into Scorpio deepens the emotional landscape of your relationships. Dive beneath the surface, explore the mysteries of intimacy, and embrace the transformative power of authentic connections. This Venusian transit encourages heightened passion.

NOVEMBER WEEK TWO

◎ Brace yourself for a groundbreaking cosmic shift as the revolutionary Uranus takes center stage in the steadfast realm of Taurus. This celestial dance promises a period of radical transformation, urging you to rethink and innovate the foundations of stability and security in your life. Embrace flexibility and welcome the unexpected, for this transit invites you to adapt to new, groundbreaking ideas that can reshape your world.

💔 The celestial drama unfolds with Venus square Pluto, delving into the profound depths of your relationships. This intense aspect serves as a cosmic catalyst, pushing you to confront and overcome challenges. Prepare for a metamorphosis in matters of the heart, where relationships undergo a powerful transformation, ultimately leading to a rebirth.

☾ The Moon gracefully glides into Cancer, infusing the cosmic scene with nurturing and emotional energy. This lunar phase prompts a deep dive into your feelings, encouraging you to prioritize self-care and connect with your intuitive, nurturing side. Find solace in the comforts of home and the warmth of loved ones during this reflective time.

NOVEMBER WEEK TWO

🔄 Mercury takes a retrograde turn, signaling a cosmic call to review and reassess. It's a period to revisit old projects, relationships, and unresolved issues. Exercise caution in communication, anticipate delays and embrace the opportunity for inner reflection.

🦁 The lunar spotlight then shifts to Leo, ushering in a vibrant and creative energy. This phase invites you to tap into your inner performer, engaging in activities that bring joy and allow you to radiate your authentic light. Express yourself creatively and let your talents shine.

🔍 As Jupiter, the planet of expansion, takes a reflective pause with its retrograde, the cosmic energies encourage you to reassess personal beliefs, philosophies, and growth goals. Use this introspective period for inner exploration and refining your life's path.

🛡️ Mercury's conjunction with Mars injects dynamism into communication and mental agility. Leverage this potent energy to express your thoughts assertively and tackle tasks with precision. However, be mindful of potential conflicts that may arise from impulsive words.

NOVEMBER WEEK THREE

✳ The Sun's trine with structured Saturn brings a stabilizing influence to your endeavors. Your disciplined efforts align with long-term goals, leading to tangible achievements. This cosmic alliance encourages decision-making and a solid foundation for success.

💬 As communicative Mercury forms a sextile with transformative Pluto, your thoughts and conversations delve into profound territory. Engage in meaningful discussions, explore deeper truths, and be open to mental transformations. This cosmic alignment empowers your words with insight and intensity.

🔍 Mercury, the planet of intellect, enters the mysterious realms of Scorpio, intensifying your thoughts and communication style. Dive beneath the surface, explore deeper meanings, and be open to unveiling secrets. This cosmic phase encourages research, investigation, and a keen understanding of hidden aspects.

🔄 Brace yourself for mental fireworks as Mercury opposes the unpredictable Uranus. Your mind is charged with innovative ideas, but be mindful of sudden changes and unexpected revelations.

NOVEMBER WEEK THREE

🌑 The New Moon marks a powerful fresh start, urging you to set new intentions and plant seeds for the future. Embrace the energy of beginnings, visualize your goals, and initiate actions aligned with your aspirations. This lunar phase invites you to embark on a journey of self-discovery and manifestation.

☀ The Sun aligns with Mercury, amplifying the power of communication and self-expression. Your thoughts seamlessly align with your sense of self, enhancing clarity in your words and ideas. It's an excellent time for self-reflection, effective communication, and expressing your authentic voice.

☿ Mercury's shift into adventurous Sagittarius expands your intellectual horizons. Embrace a broad perspective, indulge in philosophical discussions, and seek the truth. Your mind craves exploration and learning, making it a favorable time for higher knowledge and expansive thinking.

♆ The harmonious sextile between Uranus and Neptune sparks innovation with a touch of enchantment. Embrace your unique ideas, and allow creativity to flow.

NOVEMBER WEEK FOUR

🌑 The cosmic spotlight shifts as the Sun gracefully enters Sagittarius. A burst of adventurous energy, as Sagittarius' influence encourages exploration and a quest for knowledge. Your focus may turn toward expanding horizons, seeking new experiences, and embracing the joy of discovery. This solar transit ignites a fiery passion within, urging you to chase your dreams with enthusiasm and optimism. Embrace the spirit of adventure and let the cosmic archer guide you toward new possibilities.

🔗 Communication gains a touch of grounded wisdom as Mercury forms a harmonious trine with Saturn. Your thoughts and words are infused with practicality and a long-term perspective. This celestial alliance supports structured and disciplined thinking, making it a suitable time for strategic planning and organized decision-making. Use this cosmic connection to build solid foundations for your ideas and projects.

🌐 A celestial conversation between Mercury and Jupiter enhances your mental prowess and expands your intellectual horizons. Your mind is open to grand ideas, and you may find yourself drawn to learning or teaching.

NOVEMBER WEEK FOUR

💚 The harmonious trine between Venus and Jupiter creates an atmosphere of abundance and joy in matters of love and pleasure. This celestial dance encourages you to indulge in the finer things in life and to expand your capacity for love and enjoyment. It's a time to celebrate relationships, appreciate beauty, and bask in the positivity that surrounds you.

♉ The cosmic harmony between Venus and Saturn brings stability and commitment to your relationships and creative endeavors. This alignment emphasizes the importance of building lasting foundations in matters of the heart and artistic pursuits. Your connections deepen, and your creative projects gain structure and longevity under this celestial influence.

♎ Saturn, the cosmic taskmaster, resumes its forward motion, signaling a growth shift in the cosmic energies.

🔄 The cosmic messenger, Mercury, resumes its direct motion, lifting the fog of retrograde energies. Communication flows more smoothly, and any delays or misunderstandings begin to resolve.

DECEMBER WEEK ONE

☽ Feel the grounding embrace as the Moon gracefully enters Taurus, bringing a sense of stability and comfort to your emotional landscape. Taurus' energy encourages you to indulge in the pleasures of the senses and find security in the present moment. Take this time to nurture yourself and create a solid foundation for your emotions.

♥ Experience the transformative dance of love and power as Venus sextiles Pluto. This cosmic alignment adds depth and intensity to your relationships. Embrace the potential for positive changes and explore the profound connection between your heart and soul. Let the energy of love and transformation guide your journey.

☽ Transition into the versatile energy of Gemini as the Moon moves into this communicative and adaptable sign. Gemini's influence inspires curiosity and a desire for intellectual exploration. It's a time to engage in diverse interests, connect with others through conversation, and remain open to new ideas.

DECEMBER WEEK ONE

🌕 Bask in the glow of the Full Moon, a culmination of energies and emotions. This potent lunar phase illuminates aspects of your life, offering clarity and insight. Reflect on your achievements, release what no longer serves you, and harness the Full Moon's energy to manifest your intentions.

🌙 Feel the nurturing embrace of Cancer as the Moon finds its way into this watery sign. Cancer's energy enhances your sensitivity and deepens your emotional connections. Create a cozy and secure space for yourself and your loved ones, and let your intuition guide you through this lunar transition.

🌑 Engage in dreamy and imaginative thinking as Mercury forms a harmonious trine with Neptune. This cosmic alignment enhances your intuition and creative expression. Dive into the realms of inspiration, trust your instincts, and let your imagination flow freely.

🌙 Step into the radiant energy of Leo as the Moon graces this fiery sign with its presence. Leo's influence encourages self-expression, creativity, and a desire to shine.

DECEMBER WEEK TWO

💧 It's a cosmic tension as Mars squares Saturn, a celestial clash between action and restraint. Navigate challenges with patience and strategic thinking, channeling the disciplined energy of Saturn to overcome obstacles on your cosmic journey.

🌙 The Moon gracefully enters Virgo, grounding emotions in practicality and attention to detail. Find solace in the beauty of order and let the lunar energy guide you to organize your emotional landscape with meticulous care.

☾ Neptune turns direct, releasing a mystical current into the cosmic waters. Dreams awaken, and illusions dissipate as Neptune resumes its forward motion. Embrace the subtle whispers of intuition and allow the tides of inspiration to guide your creative endeavors.

⚡ Brace yourself for the dynamic dance of Mercury opposing Uranus, creating sparks of intellectual electricity. Unpredictability colors your thoughts, and innovative ideas take center stage. Embrace the cosmic lightning bolts of inspiration, but be mindful of sudden shifts in communication.

DECEMBER WEEK TWO

🪨 Mercury forms a harmonious trine with Neptune, casting a dreamy aura over your thoughts and expressions. Your words become a poetic dance, and your mind drifts into the realms of imagination.

♐ Mercury gracefully enters Sagittarius, adding a touch of adventurous flair to your thoughts and expressions. Your mind seeks expansive horizons, and your words take flight like arrows aiming for the stars. Embrace the spirit of exploration and let the cosmic archer guide your intellect toward new and exciting possibilities.

🌙 The Moon enters diplomatic Libra, infusing the cosmic stage with a sense of harmony and balance. Emotions find equilibrium, and relationships take center stage. Seek the beauty in connections, and let the cosmic scales of Libra guide you toward understanding and cooperation in your emotional interactions.

✦ Mercury sextiles Pluto, creating a cosmic synergy between intellect and transformation. Your words hold a potent allure, and your thoughts delve into the depths of profound insights. Explore the transformative power of communication during this celestial alignment.

DECEMBER WEEK THREE

◐ Mars strides into a disciplined Capricorn, infusing your actions with ambition and a strategic mindset. Your drive takes on a focused and determined quality, propelling you toward your goals. Channel the energy of Mars in Capricorn for resilient perseverance and methodical progress on your cosmic journey.

◯ The Sun squares Saturn, creating a cosmic challenge that calls for patience and perseverance. Obstacles may arise, testing your resolve. Approach challenges with a steady heart and a commitment to your goals. The celestial square encourages you to build resilience and face difficulties with determined strength.

☽ Sagittarius beckons as the Moon dances into this adventurous sign. Embrace the expansive energy of Sagittarius, and let your emotions soar into the vast horizons of possibilities.

● The cosmic canvas is reset with the arrival of the New Moon, a celestial invitation to set intentions and plant seeds of growth. Harness the energy of the New Moon in Sagittarius to envision new horizons and embark on fresh adventures.

DECEMBER WEEK THREE

◯ The Sun squares Neptune, creating a celestial tension between reality and illusion. Be mindful of potential confusion or deception in your pursuits. Ground yourself in practicality while remaining open to the spiritual realms. Navigate the cosmic waves with clarity and discernment during this square.

💝 Venus squares Saturn, casting a cosmic dance between love and responsibility. Use this celestial square to strengthen the foundations of your connections and embrace the responsibilities that come with romance.

❄ The December Solstice marks a celestial turning point, as the Northern Hemisphere experiences the longest night. Welcome the return of the light, both metaphorically and literally. Reflect on the lessons of the past and set intentions for the unfolding journey ahead.

◯ The Sun gracefully enters Capricorn, marking the December Solstice and a shift in cosmic energies. Embrace the Capricornian qualities of discipline, ambition, and a steadfast approach to your goals. Let the Sun's light guide you through the longest night, illuminating your path with wisdom and determination.

DECEMBER WEEK FOUR

💜 Venus squares Neptune, casting a cosmic dance between love and illusion. Relationships may be bathed in dreamy hues, but be mindful of potential confusion or unrealistic expectations. Ground your affections in reality while appreciating the beauty of romantic ideals. Navigate the ethereal waters of love with clarity and discernment during this celestial square.

🏛 Venus gracefully enters Capricorn, adding a touch of pragmatism to matters of the heart. Love takes on a more serious tone as relationships seek stability and commitment. Embrace the Capricornian qualities of responsibility and long-term vision in your romantic endeavors. Let the cosmic goat guide your affections with purpose.

🌙 The Moon gently waltzes into Pisces, ushering in an emotional tide of sensitivity and intuition. Dreams may weave through your emotions, inviting you to explore the realms of imagination. Allow the gentle currents of Pisces to guide your emotional landscape, nurturing your soul with compassion.

DECEMBER WEEK FOUR

◊ Aries calls for action as the Moon boldly strides into this fiery sign. Emotions become ignited with passion and a desire for adventure. Channel the dynamic energy of Aries to pursue your emotional goals with enthusiasm and courage. Embrace the cosmic warrior within as you navigate this lunar transit.

♣ The Moon settles into Taurus, grounding the emotional landscape in earthly sensibilities. Stability and comfort take precedence as you seek solace in the pleasures of the material world. Embrace the nurturing energy of Taurus, allowing your emotions to blossom like a garden in full bloom.

⊕ Mercury squares Saturn, creating a celestial tension between communication and discipline. Thoughts may face restrictions or challenges, requiring a measured and patient approach. Use this square to enhance and develop a strategy for effective communication.

☽ The Moon transitions into Gemini, bringing a breath of fresh air to your emotional realm. Curiosity and intellect take center stage as you engage in lively conversations and explore new ideas.

NOTES

NOTES

NOTES

Astrology, Tarot & Horoscope Books.

Mystic Cat

www.ingramcontent.com/pod-product-compliance
Lightning Source LLC
LaVergne TN
LVHW051844080426
835512LV00018B/3063